LANDSCAPES OF LIGHT

Poems by
B. E. Kahn

POETS WEAR PRADA • HOBOKEN, NJ

LANDSCAPES OF LIGHT

First North American Publication 2010.

Copyright © 2010 B. E. Kahn

All rights reserved. Except for use in any review or for educational purposes, the reproduction or utilization of this work in whole or in part in any form by electronic, mechanical or other means, now known or hereafter invented, including xerography, photocopying and recording, or in any informational or retrieval system, is forbidden without the written permission of the publisher. Poets Wear Prada, 533 Bloomfield Street, Second Floor, Hoboken, New Jersey 07030.

http://pwpbooks.blogspot.com/

Grateful acknowledgment is made to the following publications where some of these poems have previously appeared:

Arts and Spirituality, *Bridges: A Jewish Feminist Journal*, *Clockwise Cat*, *Lifeboat*, *New Verse News*, *Poetry Ink*, *Poetry Super Highway,* and *Schuylkill Valley Journal*.

ISBN 978-0-9841844-8-4

Printed in the U.S.A.

Front Cover Art: "Let's go to Greece," acrylic on panel, 2010, Lila Rostenberg

Author's Photo: Lynne Yellenberg

*To all those who seek the light
and to those who died in darkness.*

Contents

Greek Bus Driver Decorates His Control Panel	1
The Cypress Trees	2
High Winds—June Sailing from Oia	3
Santorini, Reflections after a Storm	4
God, How You Have Made the Blue Sea	5
Unlike Odysseus	6
Serafos	7
It Was Not Just a Pastime	8
Seascape	9
Greek and Hebrew Dance	10
Photo Taken on the Isle of Sifnos	11
Dove's Eye View	12
Immigrant Gods, Absent Address	13
At the Kotel	14
At the Kotel, Second Day	15
Is There a Way?	16
Is It Enough to Praise the Architect of the Dead Sea Scrolls Museum?	17
Questions from the Earth's Fire	18
Between Capernaum and Safad	19
"How Can You Sell A Jew for Seven Guilders?" Asks The Woman of Dutch Descent on Video at Yad Vashem	20
Until the Photo Was Developed	22
Yesterday's Shadow	23
To Be Here, My Joy	24
On Flight Number 417, Israel—Home	25
Acknowledgments	
About the Author	

Greek Bus Driver Decorates His Control Panel

I count ten talismans:
two sets of worry beads
a knitted crucifix
a metal horseshoe
and starfish
a hanging metal cross
a blue glass sphere and
indistinguishable mass
of others—a large eye of God
tiny climbing teddy bear
two saint's pictures.

On the roads through
Athens, morning and evening
traffic heavy, and routes into
Delphi, mountainous and flat—
ten times insured doesn't hurt.
Clearly, as the windshield glass
admitting light
on the subject of chance
tells us, pilgrims all—
we are the vehicle—the signs
are everywhere.

The Cypress Trees

                      spires of splendor
stand guard beneath the Acropolis.

Forged into the mountain,
exclamation points.

Fountains of tightly sprayed green,
so straight, not even bowing to

the red-roofed church dome below.

High Winds—June Sailing from Oia

A great wind sweeps this boat
reminds me to breathe.
Each crest high, higher
shouting.

We dance with it, as we skim
past mountains, island's wall.
We are foam's froth on lapis sea.
In our awkwardness

then and now we bump
out of step with waves
rhythm. Our captain
young, strong.

His arms master
ropes with first mate's help.
I cry out to You
holder of sky's cup

maker of ocean's wine.
Let us taste
gale and calm
for a while yet.

Salt thrust entwines my cells,
binds me to You. Cells, linked
from plankton to leviathan, outside-
inside ocean caves of us.

Oh wind, fill my every pore.
I am yours. I am yours.

Santorini, Reflections after a Storm

Ancient volcanic eruption—shattering
a whole land mass—more than once.

To withstand the shock, not a choice.
The earth, inhabitants—plied
their strengths, wine-pressed fruits
of encircled vines, that hugged soil
for scarce water—fused their lives.

 Still today the sea knits its safety net,
layer upon layer of healthful krill.

Wave upon wave of salt and strong
mountain's reflection—orange-gold
on aqua-blue. Myriad schools
of thoughtful fish eye each other—
octopi in tentacled embrace.

The breeze married to sun and clouds
renews breath—weaves its invisible

threads everywhere, billows the sail, stirs
the great soup until it's flavored with life.
Includes me in the mix—or I include
myself, recognizing the wind's dance
steps—one, two, one, two.

God, How You Have Made the Blue Sea

                                          so calm today,
sapphire steady—as yesterday on the way to
Sifnos—the salt air stretched, inflated the swells
twelve feet high. (I learned *sifenus*, or something
like that word, in Greek, means wind)

I heard its soft low howl, not a moan, not sad—
but cloud bellows, full of life, breath for this day.

And it met me on the road to Kastro to see ruins
of an old castle when we found Maximos,
woke him from his morning sleep—an artist
designing canvas and clay, silver and gold.

I saw on his easel the exact dream I dreamt—
of ocean, colored by volcano—after-images,
green, when the rock was red and red when the rock
was green. There it was—now, my dream—to own.

Unlike Odysseus

                      if you do not know where home is,
does the sea tell? In a song that comes to mind,
is the answer there, in the heart's listening?
how it lifts and falls, billows—its own enraptured
life jacket—knows the boat is strong, the captain, sure.

As we approach the Isle of Folegandros, an open hand
appears in the rocks—concave palm, fingers outstretched,
carved by eons. It bids me welcome, welcome as does
each person I have met here, who seeks nothing from me,
wishes only to find me not-the-stranger,
knows deep in his blood the pierce of exile's lance.

From this boat, the bright blue eyes, windows of houses
shuttered from afternoon light, now nod and wink
to sun—so too the roses and pink
oleanders planted in terraces, mortar-braced. A wall
of welcome—my heart song dissolves its stones.

Serafos

The crescent-moon-shaped road
streams down the mountain.

Serpentine stone steps echo the hills.
The workers who cemented them

painted the edges for safety's sake.
These paths silently spill time into me.

Townspeople carry binoculars. Is it
to see space spoken? Our language

differs, but smiles, gestures carry
our thoughts across the wire

of our minds. Could I live here? Would
my laughter sing in the white houses,

through painted blue doors,
seep into pots of geranium?

It Was Not Just a Pastime

        faithful Penelope's weaving.   Armies
destroy   explore   dismantle
imitate the heaving winds
inside earth's caves   erupt

into rocks of battle.   Women mend
forever   as best we can
as events skew the world   spilling   time.

We imitate too   the sea waves'
blend   a moving   tapestry
of light, fire, water. We try to
reconnect the fisher's net

seek   nourish   twine of peace
constancy   on the great loom.

Seascape

Sea griffins and mollusks
krill, plankton—Agean ocean,

aqua thrill, crimson after-image
of mountains swim in my head

fill my third eye pronouncedly
and for a long time.

                    There is
no unnatural killing of life below

the sea, brimful
of known, unknown creatures—

cyclops, sirens' call, dragons of old.
The fall and rise of rollers'

crisp song and eddied breeze
chart without outline our ship,
Aphrodite.

                    We receive her
morning showers after lulled sleep,

blue-green rhythms. We, scarfed
belly dancers, *tangeras, tangeros*

gyrate, glide into ports—
towns full of children

who sit on walls
together, play imaginary games.

Greek and Hebrew Dance

From our boat, docked on the Island of Paros, we hear sea's tongue, satisfied cat, lap at us; music wafting from close-by taverna, where outdoor diners eat fried smelt and mullet, lounge, goblets in hand.

There, Greek men dance in white costumes, black and red belts, sleeves wide as angel wings. The dancers touch each other only with handkerchiefs, like the Chasidim, but off-beat.

The songs, not like the Jewish or Hebrew dances I know. That music stamps and brushes every note—not to hesitate, miss even a waver of sound. Fringes bounce, talismans of freedom, action bound to universe.

To dance this Greek dance, I must lift heel and sole—be sure to wait for what comes next. The passion tempered by foot crossed in front of foot, by ritual, by melody. Yet all the music—Greek, Jewish, Israeli wails in minor key.

In both lands, the young dance, kick legs in air, bend to the ground. Elders watch clap, smile. The folk, the folk keep dancing, eating, singing. Accordion players play children's tunes, epics, love songs.

Music, moon late night partners.

Photo Taken on the Isle of Sifnos

The sun, great eye of heaven,
through lid and lash of cloud

searchlights its reflection, colored
cleft of sky's after image. On my photo

the brilliant gold iris mesmerizes.
Do not gaze too long at the sun.

It will blind, will blind you. This sight,
resonant as candles lit to gift the sea

and blue above. Photo tilted sideways—
sun, its reflection, a pair. Now both

stare at me, asking *What next?*
What next?

Dove's Eye View

Different from Athens and the Acropolis—
Jerusalem—*The temple is the city.*
The city is the temple. Nothing to equal
the wholeness of this blessing, this light.
ৡ

The Jacarunda, that lilac-looking tree lifts
its delicate, small spires into the air of Safad,
where, mystical fires within the souls of ancient
rabbis still weave smoke, scent into life.
ৡ

One synagogue here, five hundred years old
sits like a *kipah* atop this enraptured city.
Inside, I saw many Torah arks, even allowed
to photograph one. Result: a rainbow blur.
ৡ

Outside Tiberias, hot springs warmed my hands,
nearby volcano made manifest. We ate
St. Peter's fish, (filleted by Smuel or Ered)
sea bass, attracted by the water's holy heat.
ৡ

Today the altitudes, attars dizzy me—
Safad, three thousand feet above sea level,
poinsettias' orange-blossom aroma,
Tiberias, six hundred feet below.
ৡ

It is Jerusalem that centers me, serenely
lifts me to its heights. I feel its holy current—
always—golden light, seeped into stone everywhere,
seeped, streaming through my heart, soul, breath.

Immigrant Gods, Absent Address

Our gods, and we brought
several of them to America,

do not inhabit our mountains
in temples. We do not look up

and see their dwellings. Circled
above the horizon, no columns

Doric, Corinthian, Western Walls
on high to ease our cares, remind us

we are the underlings, though
exalted in service to them.

≈

I love this daily mountain memo
of heights in Jerusalem, Athens. Spirit

manifests everywhere. And the people
dance and say what they feel

about the dance, their lives
connected. Shrines, memorials

on the roads, candles beam.

At the Kotel

The Wall   a sea of women's prayers.   Tiny
pieces of paper tucked into cracks   weave

our hearts together   intentionally.   We navigate
narrow straits   spaces between   golden rock

holding for centuries our lives   dreams
deep hope for others   ourselves.   Tears

wash our praying upwards   past the veil
of white and lavender caper plant hanging

above me that gives blessed shade
and into the pale crevices.   These tears

moisten   revive   the lost Temple   make whole
this tapestry today.   We women

take our turns being close   so close
we hear the stones whisper   reply.

At the Kotel, Second Day

Those prayers I sent into the cracks
of light-soaked stone

are sailing somewhere in a sea
of wished-for things. Whitecaps

buffet or caress. I don't know which.
The wind's voice presents its favors.

I am grateful for the wind's
keening high and lilting low.

Is There a Way?

From the carob tree   carob seed
used to weigh gold.   Carat

our measure.   Jerusalem   city
of gold.   How do we scan its

brilliance   gauge its morning
and evening light?   The energy

paths of its inhabitants?

The pomegranate spills its seed
all over our clothes   seals them

crimson.   Hearts
flow red too.   Can we mend

the bleeding?   My friend's wise
mother said   " You should only

eat pomegranates when you are
naked."   How many ways

are there to be naked?

Is It Enough to Praise the Architect of the Dead Sea Scrolls Museum?

                      White domed sanctuary for holy writ mimics shape of ancient pottery vessel.

Noble planner, you honor the unknown, humble artisan whose skill shone in preserving these words, two thousand years.

                      The scrolls stood in the four foot high earthen storage urn in a cave at Qumran. There a Bedouin shepherd who'd lost a stray lamb

(and feared his father's wrath) dropped pebbles down into the vault to scare the creature back to its flock.

The shepherd's ear heard "riches" in the stone's twang on clay. Heartened, he found help to reach the lamb.

                      Is it enough to honor the shepherd who overcame his fear?

Is it enough to honor the stone he threw that clanged but did not break the vessel?

Is it enough to honor the help the shepherd's brother brought to raise the clay pot and its contents from the cave?

                      Is it enough to praise how we are all one—

how our talents lift mud to holy form and words to sanctity? Is it enough…

Questions from the Earth's Fire

Coastline curving—
chartreuse-scalloped sand
juts into aqua-blue.

The Dead Sea reflects
the mountains, sharply
etched white. They are

mirrored in the water
as promise—
edges blurred as cloud.

≈

Irregular seascape asks, "What is real?"
this pinkness, now indigo. Where
is it written (here in this land?)—
in histories of volcanoes erupting,
minerals heaved into the water—
to ignore earth's healing gifts?

Rather we reply, "Shall we coat our faces,
lather our bodies with mud, Arab and Jew,
so we cannot recognize, construe from
outer signs, shibboleths just
who we think we are,
slide together, expecting salt—

then enter the sea,
accept buoyancy at last."

Between Capernaum and Safad

Tall purple candles in the hills
north of the Sea of Galilee—thistle—

my Canadian friend, whose husband worked
in the garment industry—tells me, was used

to brush lint from fabric. To buy a dry
thistle (in Toronto) expensive, she said.

And I wonder if the plant were gathered here,
how many dead would it cost to make clean

new raiment? Would the ancient, holy mystics
have bled that royal color into their lives or

could they have found a way around these hills
attaining the greater heights they sought.

 How long have we fought, we good people of
The Book—to find and keep our home.

When shall the shining clothes be ours,
free of debris?

"How Can You Sell A Jew for Seven Guilders?" Asks The Woman of Dutch Descent on Video at Yad Vashem

Yad Vashem, Holocaust Museum in Israel

You don't like my silver, its shine,
brilliance—to say nothing of my gold?
Yet you looted, stole, confiscated
every goblet, crown and *yad* that points
to prayer from my Torah.

> You say you despised my portrait,
> those canvasses of my measured nose
> and skull, but you heisted, even sold them
> to museums. Forget my books, poems,
> the music you burned. It was all
> not worthy of attention, you say.

Why did you so covet that rich world,
starve me in all the ghettos as you wrung it
from me? You taught me the sewing
machine and scissors dance, but only
in dreams. Each of those—tools
you used to kill me.

> Some of us, stubborn beyond belief
> etched dole-times from our bread ration cards
> and tombstone dates of our fathers' deaths
> onto silver brooches. No gems remain—
> only street stones of emaciated echo.

I don't want to hear, far or near, those Warsaw
words. But you listen. Hear me plain.
Not ever again will you force our brains, timed

to hobble, walk only one way, on cobbled paths
at your policeman's brutal whim.

    In spite of him, our people survives, thrives.
    We pray never to have to know what today's
    traffic will bear.

Until the Photo Was Developed

> *In the Judean wilderness, Israeli farmers, growers of grapes, dates—invite Arab shepherds there to graze their sheep. Item, unreported by any press.*

In the Judean Desert
there are leopards.

One, in fact, attended
a wedding. He sat in a tree

during the whole affair.
No one knew he was there.

Yesterday's Shadow

    I pray
                      disappears
through Jerusalem's gold light.

    Garment of sheen envelops
us in space all around.

    Splayed darkness
and the knife of old sacrifice
                            gone.

To Be Here, My Joy

To breathe this sun-filled air—unannounced
to parents (as neither Messiah, scorpion,
nor husband, as folk view of Talmud describes)

I appeared—a gift—as are we all.
My right to home, though means were absent,
clear. I wandered near and distant shores

till miracle—the sea wove for me
a many colored coat from out its gentle
spectral mists. Wearing it proudly

I traveled here. And now, olive trees
and grapes abound from your good
works. The desert blooms, indeed.

Safely the sweet tents shall be lit. And
safely, safely I deserve, as do we all,
to sleep and wake, love and work
and dance in peace.

On Flight Number 417, Israel—Home

The sky, blue and white
Israeli flag reminder. We fly
out of the desert, leave
our precious fig tree
to find its place in our heart.

And we do secure our truth.
Tears proclaim
the wholeness we seek.

And we do declare our minds—
blue sky, cloudless.
Rays of light abound.

And we do see below and above us—
oceans of salt and stars' berth.
All blessings—sing, guide us—
twisted through
the bread of our gifted days.

Acknowledgments

The author wishes to thank the editors of the following journals in which some of these poems have appeared:

Arts and Spirituality, 2007	"Greek Bus Driver Decorates His Control Panel"
Bridges: A Jewish Feminist Journal, Vol. 11, No. 2, Autumn 2006	"Between Capernaum and Safad"
Clockwise Cat, December 2007	"The Cypress Trees," "Immigrant Gods, Absent Address"
Lifeboat, December 2007	"Santorini, Reflections after a Storm"
Lifeboat, January 2008	"Photo Taken on the Isle of Sifnos"
New Verse News, November 2007	"Until the Photo Was Developed"
Poetry Ink, 2006	"Questions from the Earth's Fire"
Poetry Super Highway, June 2010	"At the Kotel, Second Day"
Schuylkill Valley Journal, Fall 2008	"Is There a Way?"

I am grateful to my friends in poetry for their help with these poems. A special thanks to William Conrad for his encouragement, and to Roxanne Hoffman for her expertise and her understanding heart. Lastly, I cherish that my first trip to Israel took place in 2005, during a time of peace, with which I hope the land will always be blessed.

About the Author

B. E. Kahn, native Philadelphian, is a grant recipient of both the Pennsylvania Council of the Arts and the Pew Fellowships in the Arts. Her poems have appeared in *Harrisburg Review*, *Philadelphia Poets*, *Bridges: A Jewish Feminist Journal*, *The Mad Poets Review*, *Schuylkill Valley Journal* and the online *Tupelo Press Poetry Project*, among other publications. A retired speech therapist, she lives in Wynnewood, Pennsylvania and has taught poetry to intergenerational, interfaith groups. She is a member of the 34th Street Poets Cooperative. Her chapbook, *Spring Apples Silver Birch* was published October, 2008 by Greenleaf Press.

For more information about the author visit her website: www.bekahn.com.

About the Artist

Lila Rostenberg, born Lila Kathryn Thaxton, in Norman, Oklahoma, the eldest of four, spent much time playing in the wide open spaces of western Oklahoma. Encouraged by her family to pursue her creativity and artistic skills, she attended Henderson State University in Arkadelphia majoring in art with a special emphasis on landscape and still life painting.

She discovered watercolor after graduating, and has painted many happy hours while learning the beauty of this medium, studying at the Arkansas Arts Center in Little Rock, as well as with private teachers and on her own. She also has worked in fiber arts, quilting, knitting and weaving, "making objects which are utilitarian as well as beautiful," and teaching others as the owner and creative force behind Quilt Your Heart Out, a quilt shop in Fayetteville from 1993-2003.

She lives with her husband in Arkansas. Visit her online at http://indigopears.blogspot.com.

www.ingramcontent.com/pod-product-compliance
Lightning Source LLC
Chambersburg PA
CBHW061518040426

42450CB00008B/1685